5.95

SPIRITUAL
UNFOLDMENT

Some further books of White Eagle's teaching:

THE GENTLE BROTHER

GOLDEN HARVEST

HEAL THYSELF

THE LIVING WORD OF ST JOHN

MORNING LIGHT

PRAYER IN THE NEW AGE

THE QUIET MIND

THE PATH OF THE SOUL

SPIRITUAL UNFOLDMENT I

SUNRISE

WISDOM FROM WHITE EAGLE

SPIRITUAL
UNFOLDMENT
II

*The Ministry of Angels and the
Invisible World of Nature*

WHITE EAGLE

THE WHITE EAGLE PUBLISHING TRUST
LISS · HAMPSHIRE · ENGLAND
MCMLXXXI

First published in November 1969

Reprinted October 1975
Reprinted December 1977
Reprinted November 1979
Reprinted January 1981

ISBN 0 85487 001 6

PRINTED IN GREAT BRITAIN BY
FLETCHER AND SON LTD, NORWICH

CONTENTS

I

GATEWAY INTO FAIRY-PLACES

Thousands of years ago, the ancient peoples used to fertilise their crops literally by calling down heavenly grace, by use of angelic power. Some try to do much the same today intermittently as during the traditional rogation service in the fields, when the pastor asks for a blessing on the future crops; or even when someone with 'green fingers' quietly works in a garden he loves. The difference is that the ancients proved constant and devoted in their co-operation with the angelic powers and the 'little people' of the nature kingdom, and in calling down the Light to bless their lands. With the result, so we are told, that crops were rich in flavour and nutritive power. Today we try to grow our crops almost in defiance of nature, by means of chemical fertilisers, insecticides, and other artificial means designed to cheat nature; and in doing so we banish the fairies from our gardens and fields.

Most readers of this book have already

welcomed and accepted White Eagle's teaching, and will want to learn more about fairies, angels and the great invisible powers of earth and heaven; but a few will open it who don't, and perhaps won't believe in fairies, believing that they exist only in children's imagination, and that angels are reserved for stained-glass windows and Bible stories. We hope that they will read on, for they will find that everything in this book will presently make sense to them.

The Bible says, in a pregnant passage, that '*The dead know not anything*'—the 'dead' being those who are *dead in spirit*, unaware of anything they cannot taste, touch, hear or see. 'The dead know not anything' because theirs is a chimerical existence, spent in a world of *maya* or illusion.

The Bible compares these 'dead' with the 'quick'; the former being those who care not whence they have come, why they are here, or whither they will go after death; whereas the 'quick' are those beginning to care. Our stranger, we believe, belongs to the latter category, and as his reading proceeds, so will his process of quickening hasten. He will find these pages reveal a quality of knowledge and vision recognisable as supernormal, or as some might think, 'superhuman'; for it is a knowledge of a kind that can only be found stored in the ancient wisdom from which it comes, and spoken by messengers of the ancient wisdom.

'Why White Eagle?' our stranger reader will ask. The eagle is a bird with far-ranging vision, a creature of the heights. Symbolically the name White Eagle means a spiritual teacher, and can refer to any sage or teacher possessing the eagle's vision. St. John of the Fourth Gospel, has always been symbolically represented by the eagle. What of our own messenger bearing this symbolic name?

Those who have known him for many years have always found him gentle, unfailingly courteous, ever regardful of others' feelings. He always seems to have a complete knowledge of the soul of the one to whom he talks, to be aware of his inner self, his thoughts and feelings. To that inner self White Eagle speaks with his own gentle wisdom. The reader will sense in the messages a spiritual quality and origin; will feel they are tinged throughout by a light not of this earth, and that their speaker is no longer bound down to earthliness. Indeed, he speaks to us 'from the spirit,' from a plane (or planes) above this, where souls live that are purer and wiser than men on earth.

How then does the message come to us?

By reason of his very long association with someone capable of receiving and transmitting that message. Between these two is a link which spans the ages, and indeed, in this incarnation is lifelong.

White Eagle like others who have transcended matter or the material state, has an abiding place in the mountain heights but can also migrate at will to other heavenly planes or places.

Grace Cooke, the recipient of his message, recounts in her book, *The Illumined Ones*, how she travelled in spirit to visit White Eagle in his home in the Himalayas.

Her visit, she says, was not in any sense 'other worldly,' but homely and natural. She found White Eagle just as she had expected, gentle of speech, with a quick and ready humour, and most of all, a warm, sympathetic and loving quality which his whole mien expressed. His home was at a great height, a window of the room revealing a vast expanse of mountains reaching out to the horizon—a place above and beyond the world.

When White Eagle speaks to us, he speaks, as we have said, 'from the spirit,' although we can only guess what that term implies. This book is compiled from lectures and talks given by him through the instrumentality of Grace Cooke over a long period. Some go back as far as 1934, while others are comparatively recent. Thus they cover more than a quarter of a century; and it is noticeable that in these talks there was no contradiction in detail, only an elaboration over the years. Surely a remarkable demonstration of consistency.

If we are going to learn anything about fairies and angels, and even about White Eagle's message, it might be as well to ask ourselves what kind of universe we live in. In imagination we go out on a dark night under a starlit sky. All our visible universe is spread out, unrolled above us, bright and beautiful, albeit frightening if we contemplate its vastness, its terrible immensity. For then we begin to think how tiny, how fragile by comparison is our earth, how easily it could be annihilated and how we ourselves are only infinitesimal beings living tender and most fragile lives. We stand, frightened before the immensity of everything, by its very soul-lessness, its indifference.

Meanwhile the stars shine on unheeding. . . .

Now, we try to more quietly feel, to breathe-in their radiance, that same radiance which penetrates, permeates the air we breathe. In a sense, therefore, we are actually *breathing-in* the stars—breathing-in their essence, so that all these now have a share in our own being. That they must do so is quite a thought since it suggests that the firmament might be much closer to ourselves than we think, and certainly cannot be apart from us. Were it not for the garment or blanket of air above us and our earth, we should see our stars looking much closer, much brighter. Indeed they would be wonderful both in colour and variety, and would seem far more friendly.

Colour—here is something to think about, because we have instruments which can analyse every colour emanating from the stars, separate them, discover that those same elements which go to make all the stars are identical with those which make our earth, that the stars and the earth are sisterly in substance, so can never be wholly strangers or altogether apart. Brighter grows that brilliance coming from the stars now that our mind's-eye sees them more clearly. Bright and pure is that light which streams down to us from distances which were formerly thought immeasurable. In no way does distance seem to separate us, now we have formed a link with every star.

Now a strange and wonderful thought intrudes itself upon us. Might it be that not only *light* streams down to us from the starlands but also *life itself*; that their visible light-rays are serving as carriers or bearers of the essence of life itself that surges across space? And that light and life conjoined permeate all the universe, so that our own earth and every star rests immersed in a cosmic ocean of life? Can it be that cosmic waves and tides of life ever sweep onwards linking star to star, and that cosmic life itself is the energising force in all the universe, ever creative, ever beating against our world, like waves of a sea, yes, ever creating even man who is child of our world?

With what insistence, with what intelligence does this invisible life-force thrust itself into visible being! How inexhaustible seems its thrust to manifest itself, how inescapable! Life *must* take form or physical existence. It can manifest as ferocious insect, reptile, bird or animal; can live in the sea, conquer the air, even apparently vanquish nature itself when it takes form as man. Insistent life can take damaging, ruinous form, or else noble and sacrificial. Life can bless, life can curse. Life ever insists on existence in form, reaching towards perfection, sparing neither pains nor time nor labour to attain perfection. Like waves of the sea, life beats against our shores and men call that the coming of spring. In season, like a wave it ebbs away, and man calls that ebb-tide autumn or else disease or death.

The inner man in us all feels and responds to those waves of life from the cosmic sea. We have no name for these feelings, but dimly know that life sometimes brings us a closeness to God, and that this inkling of an incoming or indwelling life brings with it a yearning for continuation, for immortality.

We are still waiting and watching beneath the starlands, but now they have acquired a more heavenly sheen, in that they speak to us now of evolving life. By its very nature and insistence life must ever override death—this the universes all proclaim.

What does science say about all this? There are two kinds of scientists, the material-ists, and those leaning towards a more spiritual interpretation of the universe. The former believe this universe to be more or less like a machine evolving for ever and ever on its own without supervision or a controlling mind; comparable to some factory ever grinding out goods from machines automatically fed with an everlasting supply of material to grind.

The other kind of scientist has abandoned this painful outlook and asserts that on consideration the universe looks more like a great thought comprehending all things rather than a great machine, and that man himself bears a semblance to this great thought, has an affinity with it, is a microcosm of the Macrocosm—in other words, is made in God's image, might be a son or daughter of God. You will find some of these thoughts expressed in Sir James Jeans' book, *The Mysterious Universe*.

This chapter has suggested that we are all knit to the farthest star, and that its light and essence permeates us all—our body and mind, and our life itself. Sir Oliver Lodge, in *Ether and Space* suggests to us that everything, everybody, every world is composed of the ether of space; and that all creatures being of one substance, are therefore linked. Not only our physical selves, but our inner selves, our thinking-feeling selves, are something purely etheric. Our bodily, mortal selves are a modification of the ether, a slowing-down of vibration perhaps, as is all the physical world. Our bodies therefore are like overcoats which we wear for a stated period. Unlike overcoats, they burden us with demands for continuing sustenance and transport, for feeding and periods of rest, since they tire easily. When our span of years terminates we shed them, and proceed to live on in another world, not wholly strange because we visit it on many occasions during sleep. We sojourn for a period in that new world, which has also been created out of ether and seems as real and solid as this, but less drab, less wearing, less charged with trouble.

Fairies too are etheric creatures, part of an etheric world, as we are; were we not burdened and blinded by our physical self, we should see them, hear them, and believe in them. How then shall we begin to see fairies—can anyone tell us? Yes, but just telling does not always ensure you will see them. Meanwhile, here is a hint.

Let us suppose we are walking through some woodland glade on a bright sunny day, not closely watching the bushes and bracken on either side. From this hiding-place a host of unseen creatures watch us pass by—insects, birds, small animals—all shy, mostly fearful (and with good cause because their fellows have been decimated by man). Were we to scrutinise those bushes more closely, looking directly at the hiding creatures, they would disperse quickly. While we do not look too closely, they take their chance. So it is with fairies. Look directly at them and they will vanish. Behold them with our clairvoyant 'side-vision' and they may stay.

Unfortunately fairies have retreated ever further from man's vision. They do not like crops grown with chemicals and sprayed with poisons spelling death to insects and birds alike. They are hurt by the ravishing of animals by factory farming. They feel all these things. By adopting such practices modern man declares himself alien to nature, and falsifies his own nature; while nature replies to man's callousness with a series of diseases, animal and human, which cripple, destroy or debilitate.

Time was—10,000 or more years ago—when men so loved nature that they accepted and revered her as their great mother, and served her with devotion. Then it was that nature-spirits worked together with man as a matter of course in the sowing, tending and reaping of his crops. All was natural then, when fairies and angels were a part of man's daily life. No slaying of living creatures took place. Life in every form was revered; and so nutritious, so delicious was food grown in co-operation with fairies and angels that perfect health became man's heritage, and death, when it came, seemed to him trivial, a stepping onward to an even brighter, kinder existence.*

This is how men lived in the long ago; and how they will live again when their lives and thoughts become whole. It is the ravishing intellect of men today which would destroy us. That intellect, or lower mind, called 'the slayer of the real', demands that we believe that all our world is suffused by death. Thus says man's intellect, although those who can touch what is real know that it is not so. Rather it is life emergent, life triumphant which rides the skies. The resurrection of Jesus from death is an assertion, a demonstration of this. Life fills all space, and by its very nature arises out of death continually. Death may come by crucifixion, but life resurges in an everlasting process and life is the final victor.

This is the vision of our world and its firmament this opening chapter tries to put forward. We human creatures should seek to understand, to revere, to love all creation. With these thoughts we come at last close to the gate which barred us from fairyland, and rest upon and gaze over that gate. Gaze over, no more. Presently the gateway may be flung wide in welcome. They do not nowadays trust humans,

* This theme of life in the distant past is dealt with in the book, *The Light in Britain*. (White Eagle Publishing Trust).

these little people. How, for instance, can these earth-fairies, whose very nature it is to stimulate, to ensure healthy growth, tend crops dosed with artificial fertilisers and sprayed with insecticides, which decimate surrounding insect life and kill many birds? How can water-fairies go about their task when poisons drain away off the lands into streams and rivers, whence they find outlet into the sea? For in the Antarctic the ocean fish and the fish-eating birds show trace-elements of insecticides washed off faraway lands—perhaps drained down from British fields and meadows. The fairy folk of the air must perforce move high amid the cloudlands away from the air of towns and busy roadways, polluted as the air is by oil fumes and industrial waste.

We have considered the kind of welcome present-day man extends to the little people of the Earth, Air and Water. What then of the last category—those of Fire? Fire, it would seem, is still the ultimate and final cleanser, perhaps of moral and psychic wrong-doing as well as of physical. Might it not be that the frequency of fire outbreaks today, often huge and vastly destructive in effect, represents an effort by the Fire fairies to clean us up psychically and morally?

So you will see why our gateway into fairy-land creaks on its hinges, and why fairies seem hesitant and sparse to find. Yet still they abound, can still be recognised, welcomed and won over. On lonely commons, for instance, hiding in woodlands still unsullied, or on high places; on English downlands, on mountain heights where bushes, grass and plant and tree remain unspoilt, where all are pure if not wholly pure; here the fairies are still plentiful. Nor will they isolate themselves from anyone who loves them. They will draw close to those who love growing things, to green-fingered folk who tend flowers and plants. Perhaps they already watch and wait beside such people, mostly unrecognised, unseen. So recognise them, admit them to awareness. Then they rejoice. Continue to ignore them, and they may withdraw. The gateway will open to admit those worthy of admittance—those only —because the fairy people in their own way seem a little proud and particular.

So now, no more; someone wiser, gentler, with true simplicity of heart and readiness in kindness now takes over. We give way to a more profound simplicity, to a gentler kindness. In our next and succeeding chapters, White Eagle will speak.   I.C.

II

THE BROTHERHOOD OF
MEN AND OF ANGELS

We would speak to you of the brotherhood of men and angels, that great brotherhood which already exists, but which few understand or even recognise. The phrase 'the brotherhood of man' immediately brings to the lower mind the idea of social equality, the pooling of earthly possessions and dividing them equally— that is the earthly mind's conception of brotherhood. But this is not what *we* mean when we speak of brotherhood.

Men are brothers one to another through their kinship of spirit; all were sent forth from the Logos in the beginning as sparks of life; all are of the same essence, all are children of the one supreme Parent, and in this sense, no man is greater or more important than his brother. The discarnate guides and teachers who are a little higher up the mountain side look down on the battlefield of life, seeing, not the uniform of the soldier in conflict with his fellow, but the soul and the spirit within the outer covering.

They see the soul aflame. They understand the sorrows and the human weaknesses common to every living soul, and they know that in the course of evolution, all will emerge strong and radiant, victorious over the difficulties and conflicts of earthly life.

As man's spirit, the divine energising spark of life sent forth from the Logos, descends into action through the various planes of consciousness until at last it reaches the outermost, the physical, it creates about itself that body, that garment, that temple, which we call the soul. As the spirit descends on the arc, it is gaining experience, it is becoming individualised. When in its densest form, it seems entirely merged in self, in a personality which during the effort of growth has to a degree become what you call 'selfish.' Even this has its purpose, because in the end it brings about soul growth. But while in its lowest depths, immersed as it is in self, the soul seeks, as the animal does, only for its own pleasure and power.

But in the course of its evolution, when the soul begins to absorb the light pouring upon it from the Divine, it turns to climb upward again. As a submarine sunk deep on the bed of the ocean returns eventually to the surface, so from the depths of materialism the soul turns once again to the light. Layer after layer of earthiness and selfishness is cast aside as the real nature starts to assert itself, urging the soul and spirit on to become the radiant being that God intended.

The talents with which the child of God has been endowed when sent forth upon its journey from the heart of the Logos are not buried forever, for it is by learning how to use these talents that the soul advances through the spheres of light—spheres of light which are not necessarily out of reach of man on earth, for as we have told you before, you may contact them even while you live in a physical body. It is all a question of evolution. The man who is sufficiently awakened, and who has cast off several layers of the earthly mind and habits, who is no longer bound by animal instincts, begins to become aware of inner worlds of light and beauty undreamed of before. Then he is consumed by one great urge—the urge to serve God, for his awakening has brought him a glimpse of the glory of the Great White Spirit.

Then at last he knows, for his spirit now speaks clearly within him, that only in service can he truly worship. He knows that if he desires to reach the Divine he himself must help the hosts of angels in their work. In other words, he must serve the cause of brotherhood, of evolution, recognising all men as brothers, knowing that his fellow by his side is on the same quest as himself, treading the selfsame path. And so he surges forward, one with that great army of the enlightened. He no longer wants to push his brother down, while he swims, because he knows at last that his brother is attached by the very cords of spirit to himself, and that if his brother falls he himself must inevitably go with him. By the same law, if a country misuses a neighbour country, it must ultimately go down also with that neighbour.

So it is that the Light reveals to a soul the reality of the brotherhood of man.

With the dawn of that realisation, all selfish ambition and desire is finally cast aside, and the soul holds one thought, one ideal—the common good of all. You may say at this, 'But White Eagle, does not this mean personal absorption, extinction?' No, it does not mean absorption of the individual ego, but only expansion. When man once yields himself, giving all for all, instead of loss he gains the whole world, for he expands into the cosmic consciousness, reaches even to the Christ consciousness; he becomes one with the Great White Light, one with all creation.

Once let this man turn his face towards those spheres of light (which are within him as well as without), he begins to be a 'visionary,' a 'seer.' Having freed himself from the dullness of the lower mind, his vision becomes quickened, his hearing more acute. He penetrates unknown spheres, picks up on his sensitised receiver waves of sound and light which no material instrument can register. Being now sensitised he registers these light and sound waves, and becomes aware of a new world. His soul is like a butterfly emerging from a chrysalis. Never think that such a glorious dawning comes only when one passes out of the flesh, for since these glories are of the spirit, when your own is sufficiently attuned to the Christ Light you will be able to register and behold worlds hitherto invisible.

For instance, you will become aware of the life within the nature kingdom, of streams of life parallel with the human line of evolution, and working with it; of fairies, as you call them, existing not only in children's picture books, but real, and having their own purpose in the scheme of evolution. They are busy carrying the life forces to feed the plants and the trees.

If your eyes were opened, you would see some of them in merry, rushing, tumbling, rippling, falling water; these are shining water sprites; you would see sylphs or air spirits on the wing; or in the fire you would see the spirits of the fire, the salamanders.

All manifestations of life have within them a spiritual counterpart. Don't be greedy, my dears—why should man be the only spiritual manifestation on the earth plane, and all other forms but empty shells? No, if you believe that man is spirit, clothed in flesh, then you also have to conceive a nature kingdom teeming with invisible life.

Some of these nature-spirits will eventually evolve to the angelic plane, and follow a parallel line of evolution to the human. As the human will eventually become divine, so certain nature-spirits evolve from gnomes, fairies and sprites to become angelic forms. In the angelic form they play a great part in human life. You are apt to confuse the human spirit with the spirit of the angel. Make no mistake! The angels come through a different line of evolution from that followed by human kind, although it is parallel to the human line, and the angels are closely linked with man and help him in his work and life on earth. Man has always walked the earth with angels; the human race, whether it knows it or not, lives through all time under the guardianship of God's angels. It may strengthen and comfort you to know that not one of you treads the path of life alone; for from the moment of birth until physical death, you are guarded by an angel appointed for that task. Now the guardian angel is *not* the guide. The guide is human in origin, the guardian angel is angelic. Shall we call the guardian angel the guardian of the law, custodian of the karmic law which rules all life? Does not the Bible tell of a recording angel? In this progressive age you have set this idea aside as nonsense. Believe us, beloved children, the recording angel is a reality, though not in the crude sense fostered by the old teaching. The guardian of the law watches over, records and guides the outworking of the karmic law, or the law of cause and effect.

The idea of angels as winged beings is not far from the truth. Man, living in a state of semi-darkness imprisoned in the flesh, can have very little idea of the glory of an angel. An indescribably brilliant light rises from the crown of the head of one of these beings and encircles the form, a radiance which may be seen in the form of wings of light. The great angels who come to men on a special mission from what is called the Christ circle in the heavens are all thus illumined. We speak with knowledge when we tell you that from behind the dark veil of earthliness angels from heaven minister to the souls of men.

When Peter the disciple was imprisoned, God sent an angel to his assistance, and the chains which bound him fell away. Then the angel touched him and said, 'Follow me,' and the disciple duly followed. You too must learn to be alert and ready to follow the angel of the Lord, to be obedient to the voice of truth. Then, like Peter, you will be released from your earthly imprisonment, and find yourself in a world of freedom.

The angelic beings of whom we speak have never experienced human incarnation and are unable to draw very close to man until he has learned to control his emotions; but when the emotions and passions are stilled and disciplined, and the peace of the inward Christ rules, then the angel guardians can indeed come very close and protect and guide and illumine human life. Oh, if we could only make you understand and realise the beauty and the help which man can and will receive (some day when his eyes are opened) from these angelic beings whose purpose is to help him on the path of evolution and in his own service to his brother man!

Now, beloved brethren, may God bless you and give you the power to comprehend the glory of His universe. May you step forth on the path of daily duty sure of companionship and love of the angels, and of their close co-operation and guidance. So may you find that eternal peace which comes to the soul liberated from the fears of earthly bondage.

III

THE WORK OF
THE ANGELIC HIERARCHIES

Many of you are aware of the love and the guidance of friends and teachers who mingle with mankind for the purpose of serving humanity. But few realise the grandeur and the extent of the heavenly hosts concerned with life on the earth plane. You have vaguely heard about devas or angels, and have wondered if they really exist, and what is their work. You have been told also of the hierarchy who direct the plan of life and spiritual growth of mankind. Tonight at your request we shall endeavour to describe these two mighty hosts so that you may gain a more comprehensive view of the scheme of evolution.

At the outset, will you bear in mind that on the one hand are the elder brethren and the masters of the Grand Lodge who are concerned with *the growth of the spiritual consciousness in man.* On the other, there are the angelic hierarchies who are concerned with the evolution and *the building of form.*

Thus you will see that the angels are concerned with the building of vehicles or forms in every kingdom of life; and on the other hand, the masters and even greater ones beyond are dealing with the growth of the consciousness of God within the form. The plan of creation calls for the closest co-operation and interweaving of these paths, and to separate the angelic from the human is impossible. We will go so far as to say that on occasion a human soul, having evolved to the point of liberation from physical form and life, can enter the angelic line of evolution in order to work thereon. Likewise, the angels are from time to time drawn into close association with the human family.

No doubt some of you will know of the belief the ancients had that there could be union between one of these angel beings and a mortal. Do not the Arthurian legends say that Merlin was the child of such a union? This is an illustration of what we mean, that these immortal beings can mingle with man for a special purpose. But this only applies to those who have a special and high mission.

This world is very dark compared to those realms of light and beauty beyond the earth.

None can form any idea of the grandeur and beauty of the infinite scheme, nor have you any conception of the life which is evolving on other planets, closely connected with the creation and evolution of the earth. From these spiritual planets, or, as some call them, 'sacred planets,' angels come to assist in the building of form on earth.

Angel beings came to earth from Venus to assist in the beginning of this earth planet, and in the creation of the form-life on this earth. As time passed there came also to the earth those *human* beings who, having reached a certain stage on the path of evolution on another planet, were more advanced than souls then incarnating on earth. These more evolved souls assisted the younger ones on earth. Thus there came the two types of beings concerned with the creation of the earth life. There were the angels or the great planetary beings, who may be referred to as Gods; and those advanced in human evolution—God-men.

We have many times referred to the Three, who have always been since the beginning; Who are concerned purely with this solar system and the evolution of the earth planet, and Who are best understood as the three aspects, Wisdom, Love and Power. These are the Three from Whom all life comes—the three first or major Rays of life. On one of these three Rays comes the angelic line of service, concerned with life in form throughout *every* kingdom.

For life, pulsation, even growth, exists in the mineral kingdom as well as in the animal kingdom. There are those called 'elementals' who work within the mineral under the direction of angels, each assisting in his own particular way the growth and evolution of the mineral and stone. They are instruments on the invisible planes to carry life force. The most delicate subtleties of life and growth are conveyed by such tiny forms of life in the mineral kingdom.

So also in the vegetable kingdom. You who love to grow flowers, knowing that planetary influence affects the growth of flowers and herbs, may do much to assist the nature-spirits and fairies in their work. They come directly under the influence of angelic beings concerned with the growth and development of form on the earth. Great advances will be made when farmer and gardener begin to understand the influence of the planets on growing things. It is quite possible for the gardener or farmer so to attune himself to the angels and fairy kingdom as to work in co-operation and partnership with them to produce the very finest and best results.

We would emphasise the wisdom of the great ones, the elder brethren who care for the earth life. You look out on the chaotic conditions in the world; you note that human life appears to be storm-tossed, and you wonder what will be the end. Behind every department of human life, behind statesmen and governments are greater minds working for the evolution of the race. And when you see what appears to be a catastrophe, bear in mind that even here the master is at work, as a gardener with his pruning knife, and although you may have intense sympathy remember that the masters and the angelic ones have a far deeper sympathy and love for all who suffer than you can comprehend. So be at peace, recognising at all times the angelic organisation behind the scenes working always to bring the race to perfection.

A certain line of angelic creation is concerned purely with the soul of things, with the attributes both of the soul of men and the soul of the universe. Divine attributes such as love are served by the angels of Love; divine truth by the angels of Truth; divine mercy by the angels of Mercy. These angels are actually created from soul-attributes, and such angelic beings sometimes take human form, or at least wear a human face. In this is a great truth. God has made man in His own image. It seems that the human is an ideal form through which God can manifest on earth, and humanity has been shown the most perfect manifestation in Christ as the highest *ideation* of God in man, and in us all. Every form in the nature kingdom and in the angelic world and even planetary beings in some degree assume that same form.

O, my brethren! If only humanity could realise how significant is this—that man and woman are created in the image of the divine Father God, of the divine Mother God! Can you not recognise the significance of the innate divinity of humanity? Remember this when you look out upon the apparent degradation of humanity, and instead of condemning, rather worship the divine image in your brother, your sister.

One of the oldest symbols discovered on the stone carvings throughout the ancient world is the cross within the circle, symbolic of man within the universe, reaching out to give; it is symbolic of the Christ man, man made perfect, in an attitude of complete surrender and giving, held within the circle of universal love; and on his heart blooms the rose of love. But behind the cross are also the four divisions, representing the four great gods or angels of the four elements.

These are the four of the angelic hierarchy at the head of the plan of evolution of this world, four great Lords of Karma.

Under the great Lords of Karma there are other groups. They descend in the scale of evolution as does humanity. There are lords of world karma, or national karma, and of group and individual karma. The great ones have in their care and under their will, their wisdom and their power the very crust of the earth. Scientists may think all is governed by certain natural laws. And indeed this is so, but it is not the whole truth; there is an Intelligence at work behind the operation of natural law and behind the happenings and catastrophes which take place. These happenings occur by the wisdom and the will of the Lords of Karma— the gardener with the pruning knife, and are part of a vast plan for the growth and development of the human soul, covering ages of time.

In this connection we would explain that angels present during healing ceremonies are not only concerned with this life, with the healing of some particular disease. They have perfect love and compassion for their lesser brethren, but behind any individual ministration there is always the greater and broader plan of building. When the angels help to purify and perfect the physical body, they do more than this; they create, they weave into the subtler vehicles and into the actual physical form, forces of light and spiritual power destined slowly but surely to create and make ready the human form for the next race.

Do you see how beautiful is the plan for the development and evolution of man's life on earth?

Never make the mistake of thinking that the human family is the only line of life, nor the finest. But at the same time realise that in ages yet to come, in some unimaginable future, *you*, plain Mr. Brown and Mrs. Smith, may become God-men, working with the angels to create more perfect life on another planet. What a vista of eternal progression lies before you! Therefore we say, lose no opportunity to raise and quicken your soul so that it may share, with angels, in an undreamed of future.

IV

ANGELS OF LIGHT
AND DARKNESS

There are two aspects of life called respectively good and evil. On the one side, the good, are many beings working under the direction of our Lord and Master Christ. On the other are hosts who are called evil, or angels of darkness, who, although their work is different from the angels of light, are still working within the law of the cosmos, God's law. If you accept God as a Father of infinite power, you must recognise that what is called evil (or that which comes within the sphere of the angels of darkness and destruction) is yet within the hand and under the control of the Infinite Power. Otherwise there would be absolute chaos; otherwise you could have no faith, no confidence, no trust in that divine love which has been preached to mankind through the schools of mystery teaching, which in their turn have fed the religions throughout the ages. Always there has been revealed to the true pupil of the master an infinite love, guiding, protecting, inspiring and bringing good out of apparent chaos.

But surely, you say, if there are both angels of light and angels of darkness constantly at work, this must mean that conflict will never cease? It is all a question of one's conception of light and darkness. We are inclined, do you not think, to lay too much stress on darkness as something *opposed* to light? When we rise in spirit above the level of the earth we are surprised to learn that light and darkness are actually one, that conflict ceases and harmony reigns supreme, because light and darkness are reflections one of the other. Life cannot go on without darkness, which is necessary to evolution, providing as it does the negative aspect to set off the positive.

But you will not let us off with this! You will say, 'But are there *really* angels and forces of darkness? Is God the creator also God the destroyer?' Yes, in a sense this is so. The God of darkness can be likened to Shiva of the Hindus—the destroyer; but that destructive element proves itself in reality to be constructive; the destroyer which sweeps away unwanted growths is actually preparing the way for rebuilding, for re-creation. The angels of darkness therefore have their place in the great scheme of evolution.

We would draw your attention to the importance of balance. These two aspects, light and dark, positive and negative, are working together to bring about balance and equilibrium, which is one of the fundamental laws of life. The ultimate is absolute and perfect balance within the microcosm, within the Macrocosm. Thus, two aspects of life, good and evil, seen from the higher state of consciousness are two forces working together to produce the perfect life, as well as producing in the individual life the power of mastership. All men in due time will understand how to combine the positive and negative forces and blend them perfectly, so that they are working together to bring about the golden age.

We must establish this firmly and clearly in our minds; that while the angels of light are working under the supreme command of the Lord and Master of Light who is Christ the Son, the angels of darkness also are working within the law and under the command of God. But their work is complementary to that of the angels of light. These two forces are playing upon humanity with a definite purpose to bring about evolution, to bring man to the consciousness of his own innate godliness. For in the beginning, the human spirit, the individual spark of divine life was breathed forth from God to descend through many stages of life until it became clothed in matter in order to learn to control matter, and so that the divine spark of unconscious godliness might grow into a God-conscious being. You have the example of man perfected in the divine consciousness in Jesus the Christ.

Before humanity was sent forth upon this path of earthly experience, advanced beings came to this planet to assist mankind to become established on earth. Helping also with this process were angels of light and angels of shadows, principalities and powers of both good and evil. Let us restate the last sentence, saying 'angels *in* the light, angels *in* the shadows, angels serving the light and angels serving the darkness.' The angels of light (or 'good') stand for the forces of construction; those of the shadows (or 'evil') the necessary forces of destruction—necessary, because they are ever at work pruning away those aspects of individual and national life and thought which have outgrown their usefulness. Therefore do not think of the light and the dark angels as adversaries constantly at war, but rather as the one being the complement of the other. Neither underestimate the power of these beings, for both aspects of angelic life are continually at work, through generation after generation, cycle after cycle of earth's humanity, to assist the growth and destroy that which is unworthy in man.

The question then arises in your mind, Can the angels of darkness, these angelic forces perhaps not yet fully aware of the light and the power and the wisdom of the Most High, triumph over the angels of light and thus cause the destruction of humanity? Our answer is no. The dark angels can go so far and no further because then they are caught up in a cosmic law which renders them powerless. God does not allow the universe to slip out of His hands. Nothing can happen outside the will of God.

Two paths lie before man on earth, and he may choose which one he takes. On the one hand he can work in harmony with cosmic law: the man who has attained the vision of the heavenly mysteries always works in harmony with cosmic law, with the law of love. On the other hand, he who is still in a state of darkness, works, albeit unconsciously, against the cosmic law. Consequently he surrounds himself, through incarnation after incarnation, with suffering. But as soon as man learns to live and work in harmony with divine law, and to give himself confidently to God—then he attains happiness. The angels of light work with him, and he with them, and together, man and angel are able to assist in the unfolding of God-consciousness in the rest of humanity.

Remember then that as well as the invisible presences, invisible beings, there is also that within every man which is both positive and negative, white and black. What must be remembered is that mankind holds within its heart the balance. It is of vital importance that this balance between the positive and the negative should be kept. Negative thought can weigh the balance down too much on the dark side. Positive good thoughts are needed to maintain the balance as it should rightly be held in your world. The invisible beings drawn to mankind to help forward human evolution take their keynote from humanity. Equilibrium is the law.

We would hold before you a vision of the archangel Michael standing in all his sun-glory, armed with the shining sword of light. Why do we say 'sun-glory'? Because the arch-angel Michael is one of the sun spirits, a messenger from the sun, from the sphere of the Cosmic Christ; and the sword which he wields is that of spiritual truth, which Christ indeed places in the hand of every one of his followers; it is the sword of the truth of the spirit, or the son of God dwelling in every human breast. This is the weapon which will guard man through every crisis of his human life, enabling him to overcome and put aside every obstacle and every enemy. The archangel Michael is he who leads the hosts, the forces of the light.

At the start of this new age of brotherhood, the new age of Aquarius with its vast potentialities for destruction as well as progress, it is necessary for all who understand the power of the light to call upon the angels of the light, and to give their allegiance to the archangel Michael and all his angels, so that the white light may maintain the equilibrium and bring mankind into that golden age which is waiting to manifest on earth.

V

COMPANIONED BY ANGELS

We greet you, brethren. We would bring you more than our love; we would bring you wisdom and a power which will help you to realise the presence of the invisible hosts of light now ministering to humanity. Remember that however insignificant you may consider yourself to be, you can still be a channel, an instrument through which the Christ-light can manifest. Perhaps you have been brought to this present condition so that you may be used to serve. You must stand firm and loyal for what you know is truth. This truth is that the Great White Light of Christ is the healer of all conflict and of all the ills of man's body and soul. It can heal man's physical body; but more, it is the great solvent of all the problems and suffering brought about by what you call evil. Evil is the destroyer, but this Light is ever the builder, the constructor; and you who listen to and read our words are called to serve, to action by the invisible hosts.

'But how can I serve?' I hear you ask. By training yourself to become *aware* of this stream of light from God which enters your being through the psychic centres or chakras. You must become increasingly aware of this stream of life and light which, circulating through your whole being, should vivify and glorify body and soul, and then directed by your highest self, pass onwards from you to heal the sick in mind and body and soul, throughout the world.

You must understand that the angels and great spiritual beings have to work through human channels in order to build heavenly powers into the consciousness of man. This is ancient wisdom. By reason of the light awakening within the soul, the ancients became aware of the land of light, and of all the finer vibrations which affected their body and soul. They were taught how to attune themselves to the first great Cause—the Sun; how to become in harmony with the Sun and with its light; and to develop the attitude of mind that wished no harm to any living thing. The pupil thus made himself a channel; he absorbed a light which vivified every centre or chakra in his body, and through these centres, entered and illumined the seven vehicles of man.

This mystical number 'seven' is fundamental not only to man's own body, his temple, but to the entire universe. There are seven Rays of Life within which all creatures live and have their being. At the head of each Ray is one of the great Masters of the Wisdom; and behind these are the angels and archangels round the throne of God. From each Ray come forth another seven, and from each again yet another seven, so that behind and within the veil of physical life are countless hosts of beings, both of the human line of evolution and of the natural and angelic. The life within every growing thing is brought into manifestation, sustained and fed by these countless hosts.

When you look up at the night sky, and gaze at the myriad stars, you think you are looking on a whole universe—but you know nothing of the unseen life within that universe. Physical eye cannot see nor physical brain comprehend the immensity of that invisible universe. Yet if you are learning to enter the stillness within your own heart temple, you can begin to understand; to become aware of that vast invisible universe.

If you will walk in your garden in this state

of inner stillness you will become aware of other creatures, apart from man, apart from the animal and from the vegetable world. Be still; withdraw into your temple of silence. If only for a flash, you may see numberless little nature-spirits, flower fairies, gnomes. Even the very stones are inhabited by etheric folk. Yet in the ordinary way all you see is the outer form of flowers. If you stop to think, you will wonder how the flowers are brought to blossom, what brings their perfume, what is it that makes one flower yellow, another pink, and the leaves green. What power lies behind?

Behind all nature are beings great and small working under the direction and control of an angel on one of the seven Rays. These beings work automatically under their group angel—although they have a degree of choice and latitude, and they are continually carrying life force to beautify the form and colour of your flowers.

Exactly the same process takes place in every department of life. Your physical body is in the charge of what your psychologist describes as the instinctive mind, or what we have referred to as the automatic mind. Sleeping and waking, these functions go on and are controlled by the instinctive mind, which in its turn is *under the control of a great angel being*. Angels attend you from the moment of conception until the time when the silver cord is cut and you leave the mortal coil for a span, to return for refreshment to the heaven worlds.

When you are refreshed, and it is seen that the time is ripe for you to return to the vineyard, you return to incarnation to do some more work, to labour again on the spiritual path. How you labour is your own choice, but you must live always with this thought, 'I have come to the earth to serve life, to serve the grand scheme of the evolution of mankind.' You live and move and have your being in a spiritual universe, and have your part to play in it.

We endeavour to help you to increase your awareness of the angel beings. Some are assisting you to become more conscious of the glorious powers with which God has endowed you, and to become conscious of the power of God Himself. Others are working, building with the material which you offer them through your thoughts and aspirations.

We want you to realise that your thoughts are drawn by magnetic attraction towards other thought streams either positive or negative. All your positive thoughts—by this we mean uplifting, constructive thoughts—by the law of attraction join great streams of thought which are good, which are of the White Light. Negative, unkind or cruel thoughts are in their turn used to swell the great streams of darkness. Oh, how much unconscious cruelty there is! Thoughtlessness can cause much suffering, and is therefore a form of cruelty. On the other hand, your thoughtfulness and kindness, whatever form it takes, is a contribution to that great stream of White Light upon which humanity is depending for its very existence. You can contribute to it by your thoughts; and all that you withhold is robbing humanity of life—of *air* if you like.

What a responsibility rests on those who know this truth! Think of these things, and resolutely determine to give love and light to the great ocean of life. Resolve here and now that you will never fail to give the right thought, the right emotion, the right feeling to life and all your brethren.

The Great White Lodge consists of seven rays, seven colours, seven tones, seven great streams of life which pervade and permeate the earth and the worlds above, reaching out to link with the seven planets around the earth.

You contain within your body the corresponding vibrations of all these seven rays; you contain within yourself the whole universe. In some far off time you will become a centre of Light, even as God Himself. Today you are the tiniest speck; in unimaginable time you will be yourself a universe.

Is not life grand and rich? Is it not worth every effort to gain mastery, and use your God-given powers? Never think that you are alone, or that you can live to yourself; for all around you are great ones, not only of the human but also of the angelic kingdom.

In the quietness aspire to become aware of these angelic presences; strive to hear the music of their love, and to see the glory of their raiment. May your imagination reveal to you the glorious form of your own guardian angel, that messenger sent by God to help you through all the experiences of your life on earth. For each one of you has not only a human companion or guide in spirit, but also a guardian angel who comes from heavenly states of life, from supernal states and has you in his/her care. Many, many times does your guardian angel draw close, but it is only in its tranquil moments that the soul is receptive to the ministry of angels. Often you are so concerned with the world and with yourself that you are deaf to the promptings of your guardian angel.

Man of course has been given freewill choice. Every time he responds to a good, to a spiritual impulse, he is helped by his guardian angel. No effort you make to reach high, to respond to that higher influence, is ever wasted; but remember that in the degree the soul responds to heavenly influences and thereby advances on the path, it will also find itself facing human problems, and the difficulties of human relationships. Man can react to those human relationships guided either by the higher spiritual impulse, or by the instincts of the lower self. If he responds to the higher spiritual impulse, that pure light from heaven can help him to be kind, tolerant, patient and faithful—all the qualities that the soul needs in order to become in time the perfect son of God; but all this must be by his own decision, his own freewill.

We want you to recognise these two aspects —the angelic guidance, the angelic help; and the human guidance, the human help—with man himself as the principal actor, because it lies with him whether he will accept or reject such help. The guardian angel is the helper of the soul *when it desires to be helped*, by guiding it, by strengthening it.

All the important events in a man's life are attended by angels. The guardian angel, as well as the form, the influence of Divine Mother, is always present at the time of birth. Always the guardian angel cares for that soul reincarnating, and the Divine Mother's love is helping the process of that physical birth. The birth even of the smallest creature is a heavenly manifestation of an invisible power and is attended by angels.

You are perhaps unaware of what is being created when you listen to beautiful music. You love harmony; you enjoy music and rhythm with your mind, but music does something more; it affects your whole being. Few understand the soul influence of music, that it draws to the listener Angels of Music who have a work to do with the evolution of man.

Throughout the world seven tones vibrate linked with their equivalent rays of colour, and each allied to a great Angel of Music. For the moment can we transfer you to the sphere of music in thought? Can you close your eyes, imagine yourself raised to a sphere of perfect harmony listening to divine music played as by some great angelic orchestra, and see intermingling with angelic forms the most heavenly colours revealed, vibrant and actually creating life itself.

Angels of Music draw close to those who call on them. When you know how to call on these angelic beings they can pour into you creative power, which enables you to express more readily the music of your soul. So also with literature and painting, or with any of the creative arts.

Angels draw close too when ritual is exactly performed. We are speaking of course of pure and white ritual. The Angels of Ceremonial and Ritual come to assist in the building up of power at great ceremonies. They work with the higher, finer ethers, building these into form, and bringing through beauty to humanity from the creative spheres of life. Some of you may have actually seen the Angels of Ceremonial distributing power to the waiting souls of men. In the ceremonial of the Church, for instance, an angel or angels is present who, unknown to the waiting congregation, gathers the power and directs and uses it according to divine law.

At a marriage ceremony, when there is true spiritual aspiration and correct and spiritual ritual is performed (which of course takes place in the soul as well as on the outer plane) again angels draw near.

Then again there are the Angels of Healing. In every healing room an Angel of Healing is present. If you entered a sanctuary consecrated and blessed by these angelic beings, and you looked with your inner eyes opened, you would see an angel form, arms folded as if in repose, standing guard over the sacred place. These Angels of Healing carry and distribute the healing power, for they possess an inner knowledge which the human mind is unable to grasp and use. Do not run away with the idea that in your contacts with the unseen you touch only discarnate *human* souls. In your healing, the cosmic rays of colour and light are drawn upon by the angels and directed upon the patient, and the distribution, direction and infusion of these invisible rays of healing power is wonderful and interesting indeed. The healer feels the power of certain rays pouring through his hands—he feels something, he knows not what it is, and thinks he is used by his guide. Yes, so it may be, but if his eyes were opened he would see the Angel of Healing from whom these rays come.

The Angels of Healing work under the Christ-ray, under the Master Jesus. They are full of compassion, and very radiant to look upon. Some are clothed in one particular colour, others in many colours. Sometimes a group will come purely on one individual colour ray, and sometimes the group will wear pure white, bearing with them an indescribable harmony and perfume.

Try to picture a great ray of light coming down, full of angelic forms—a ray of gold, a ray of rose, a ray of soft amethyst, a ray of pure yellow, all the purest colours of the spectrum. Visualise in that ray countless forms, each with the semblance of a human face, ministering angels who work with the cosmic rays to bring healing light and comfort to the human soul and body.

When absent healing is practised, a contact is made when the patient's name is called. Men think always in terms of space, but in the soul world there is no separation by distance. Once contact with the patient is made that patient is *there*, in their midst. The angels see exactly what is wrong, the sitters are contributing their power also, concentrating on, say, the violet ray, but are a little hazy about the exact shade. What happens? The angels, being wise, can draw the required colour, a little from each of the sitters, and blend and direct to the patient exactly the ray that patient can stand, no more and no less. The angels manipulate and use the healing substance which you can give forth from your mind and heart.

This healing work is of the utmost importance, for by working with the angels, by preparing the channel, and providing them with the necessary vibrations of thought, you are helping not only individual patients, but the whole evolution of humanity.

Lastly the moment comes when man has to 'die' as you call it. But of course the real man never dies; the spirit, and the soul which clothes it, is gently withdrawn and passes out through the head, leaving the physical body like an empty shell. Again in the heavenly state, angels wait to receive the new-born soul. The Angel of Death is present at every passing, whatever may be the manner of the passing. The soul is caught up by the angel and is gently borne into the spirit life. Usually the newly born soul is like a babe, for the passing from the physical state to the next state is similar to birth into this physical life; the little form is built up above the dying physical body and is enfolded in the love of the Angel of Death. Wrapped in the comforting robe of the Angel of Death, it is borne away to its new state of life, where other angels wait to minister to it and gradually awaken it to awareness of its new life. Sometimes death may appear accidental to you, but not to the great ones, the Lords of Karma, who know exactly when death is drawing near, and prepare accordingly.

The Angel of Death is not a gruesome spectre as imagined, nor yet cold or cruel. Draw aside the veil of the Angel of Death, and you will see a face of ineffable mercy, pity and love revealed.

We would like you to understand that all life is held in God's love, and preparation is made for all the important events in man's life. We would have you think of the Great White Spirit as One Who ever loves you. Remember, children, that God, your Father–Mother–God, will never, never, forsake you. Jesus said, 'Even the very hairs of your head are numbered,' and 'Not a sparrow falls to the ground without your Father in heaven . . .'. You are held closely to His love and in the care of His ministering angels. Ask, seek, and you will receive in full measure blessings both spiritual and physical, for this is Divine Law in operation. Divine Law never fails.

VI

FAIRYLAND

It seems strange to some, to whom even the idea of the existence of the human soul beyond death is new and barely acceptable, to be told of a vast company of non-human beings whose life interpenetrates this earth life, and who are helping onward the great plan of spiritual evolution. This unseen life is behind all physical manifestation from the very lowest degree of life, upward through the spheres to the very highest. Not only is this unseen life affecting every living form, but it is also linked to life on other planets. There is no such thing in all creation as splendid isolation; there is in reality no separation between the various forms of life, for all are interdependent, and all blend in one harmonious whole. Even what appears to be error, what seems to you to be evil, destructive, serves a purpose in the great plan, and has behind it the power, wisdom and love of God which is working throughout the universe to bring good out of apparent evil; which is guiding and unifying all forms of life from the least to the greatest.

You are all familiar with fairy tales which tell of the little people who inhabit the woods, or of mermaids in the sea. Some people say they have actually seen etheric forms riding in the foam of the sea waves, and it has even been known for such forms to be photographed. We believe it true to say that the forms of fairies have also been photographed. All down the ages folk-stories and folklore have vouched for the reality of fairies, and when we go more deeply into these things you will begin to understand the true meaning of these stories and the real effect the invisible worlds have had upon man's life and spiritual development.

These little people must have been seen literally by thousands of people over the centuries, for stories about them have come down to us from Egypt, China, India, Greece, from Scandinavia especially, and from your own past. Every country of the world has its fairy folklore, and most of the stories tell much the same tale about the little people.

You in Britain owe much of your folklore and your fairy stories to Scandinavia or the northern countries of Europe. Think about this, because from the north also comes a heritage of great spiritual knowledge. When much of the earth was plunged into darkness many centuries ago, wise men withdrew to live in the Hyperborean or northern region. This again has a mystical meaning, which we will not go into more deeply now, but we want to make the point clear that from the north man has inherited a wealth of spiritual knowledge wrapped up in folklore, fairy tales and mystery teachings.

Some of you have wondered at what level or degree nature-spirits live. We would like to explain that these beings of the natural kingdom materialise or take form in the ether. You are familiar with the four elements of earth, air, fire and water; and within these four, permeating these four, is an ether finer than air. The air you breathe can be registered, weighed, analysed, but there is also an 'air' composed of finer ether. So also with water and fire and earth. Permeating the physical substance of each element is a finer corresponding ether, and from this ether nature-spirits are created, so that they belong to the etheric world in which they function, from which they come.

You look at the flowers, you inhale their perfume and exclaim, 'How beautiful!' But do

you ever wonder what lies behind and within
the flowers? You say they are manifestations of
God's love. Of course—all life is a manifestation of God's love. But how has this manifestation come about? By what spiritual process has
the flower taken form—surely there must be an
army of unseen servers who help to give form
to these manifestations of God's love? You say,
'God created the world; He created man.' Yes,
but He needs millions of workers to execute His
will. God is the Great Architect, but He has a
myriad workers, ranging from the lowest to
the highest.

Before we describe the work of these little
spirits, we want to differentiate between nature-
spirits of the four elements and those which are
called elementals, which are created *by thought*,
from elemental essence. There are many such
elementals moulded and created by thought.
This will perhaps help you to understand the
importance of man's thinking. You little realise
what you create by impure and violent thought,
or by thoughts of fear and depression. Sometimes people say that they have had undesirable
spirits near them—and it is difficult for us to
explain that these undesirable spirits are nothing but creations of their own thoughts.

The spirits known as fairies—the little fairy-spirits at work in your gardens, usually take no notice of humans, but they do respond to harmonious and loving thoughts directed to them, and in this way a human being can win the love of these little fairy creatures so busily working behind the scenes with the spiritual life essence of the flowers, the plants and the trees. These etheric creatures take varying forms, but they usually have some human likeness, and are often winged. They may be tiny indeed, or of considerable size, according to the particular work they have to do, and can be seen by the clairvoyant in any garden, in the woods, in the water, and sometimes on the domestic hearth. These latter are little spirits of the fire-element, or salamanders; they, along with any other fairy creature, can be very mischievous if provoked—so much depends on the human who attracts them. If you believe in these little people, if you love them and try to live and work in harmony with them, they will love and serve you.

There are, of course, creatures who serve the black magician; but they do not come within our category at this point, when we would present only the beautiful and positive side of the nature kingdom, although as we have already said, all are within the hand of God.

Let us return to the four elements, through which are represented four types of nature-spirits. The *earth* nature-spirits are known by many names, but we will group them under the general heading of gnomes. The *air*-spirits we will call sylphs, the *fire*-spirits, salamanders, and the *water*-spirits, we will call undines. But contained in these four groups, many variations, many different kinds of nature-spirits are at work, each with their own particular task.

Nearly all nature-spirits have power to change their size and appearance almost at will. Sometimes for a specific purpose they will enlarge themselves, but can also reduce their size and indeed can do almost anything within their own element, but they cannot change into another element. For instance, gnomes, concerned with earth, cannot merge into the air-element, nor yet the water or the fire. They live and move and have their being within their own ether, perhaps for as long as a thousand years. They are not, however, immortal; and this is where they all differ from man and from the higher line of spiritual beings or creation known as angels. The angelic messengers who minister to man and who hold power over the elementals are indeed immortal, but not the little nature-spirits. When the fairies' work or function is complete, after a time the fairy will be absorbed again into the ocean of spirit life. They do not remain individualised as the human does, or follow the same pattern of growth.

These tiny nature-spirits are not exactly separate from the angels. The little forms, labouring to carry vital force to the plant, root and flower, are animated by the thought-power of the lower angels, and so are themselves thought-forms—some people call them 'elementals'; and as we say, when their work is finished they quietly fade away. But not all fairies belong to this category for some are independent creations of their own line of evolution and work upwards to merge eventually into the angel kingdom. It is possible to help such nature-spirits up the path of evolution through human love and kindness and goodness.

Shall we now speak about the gnomes? In appearance they are usually like little dwarf men but as we have said, can change their appearance at will. Gnomes live inside the earth, and are mainly concerned with the development of the stone and mineral veins within the earth. We know well that geologists have a different explanation, but remember they have not the whole story. We tell you from our knowledge that these gnomes are concerned with the earth-element, and with the formation and creating of jewels. Fairy stories which tell about the little people with their treasures of jewels stored away in caves, are founded on truth. Such places do indeed exist inside the earth.

There is another kind of creature, busy with the earth's *surface*, who is known to inhabit the trees, the bushes, grasses and other plants. These little people are often dressed in the materials which they create, again from semi-physical earth-ether in which they exist. The gnomes frequently wear long beards, with caps on their heads, and have long, tight leg-coverings, and will be clad in jerkins or tunics, often with a band round the waist.

Those of you who have seen the little people know that they are mostly kindly and friendly towards humans, and will help them. But they will not co-operate with humans who are purely self-seekers, and get very cross if people seek to misuse fairy power. They respond well to love, so it is good and wise to send them thoughts of love.

The elementals dwelling within, inhabiting the trees, will of course look much bigger than say the gnome whose home is the plant. It is possible for the spirits to grow to a great height at will. Do you remember the story of the little girl who drank a certain potion and at once became very tall? Much frightened, she then drank another potion and became very small. These stories do not originate altogether in man's mind, although it may appear so. Most fairy stories take their origin from the fairies themselves.

By the way, the little gnomes can marry and live a kind of family life. They also eat food, not of any kind that you would understand, but food composed of their own element. They have a king and queen ruling over their colonies. The gnomes have also a substance they use, looking something like alabaster, but transparent, of which they build their palaces. You have all heard stories of children being taken *into* the hillside, into a fairy palace apparently built inside the hill. Such things do exist but are *within* physical matter and because of this you cannot see them; but when you have developed true vision, clear vision, you will then be able to see these fairy palaces in the earth. Much the same applies to similar wonders in the air and in the water. Some water-spirits have been described as mermaids. They really exist but are *within* physical matter, and therefore cannot be seen with ordinary eyesight. When a sailor declares that he has seen a mermaid he is laughed at, but what has really happened is that for a flash that sailor has had his vision unveiled and he has been able to see into the water-ether and there behold his mermaid.

Children, having recently come back from the spirit-world, are still quite close to it, and have the memory of the spirit-world and the nature-spirits still fresh in their minds. This is why they can more easily see into the fairy kingdom than can those who have been longer in earth conditions.

The undines or water-spirits are beautiful to look upon; they are graceful little creatures composed of the finer water-ether, often seen riding the waves of the ocean, or resting in rocky pools where ferns and flowers grow, or on marshy land. These water-spirits are clothed in a shimmery substance looking like water, and shining with all the colours of the sea, with green predominating. The work of the undines is with plants growing under the water and with the motion of water. They are also connected with the water-element in man's own nature, or with the emotional or soul-reactions inherent in man. When emotions are violent, these nature-spirits come crowding in, causing confusion and sometimes an emotional storm. The only power which can control that storm is that of the master of love, as when Jesus stilled the raging waters. These elementals are also real creatures willing to work with man, who can obtain both service and help from them. But if he gives way to passion he is likely to attract violence in return.

The smaller undines usually show themselves as winged beings that men call fairies, and are to be found near flowers that grow in watery places. They are very lovely, with their gossamer wings and gossamer clothing. Sometimes in a mist a little will-o'the-wisp will be seen, usually near to some marshy place or on a moor, and is composed of watery-ether—somewhat like an animated wisp of fog, it hovers from place to place. There is, we know, a scientific explanation for this phenomenon, but as we have already said, there is more than physical reason for such phenomena, and the scientific explanation does not alter the truth of what we say.

Now we come to the air-spirits, which we call 'sylphs,' and which live within the air-element. It has been said that the air-spirits much dislike being disturbed by machines tearing through the air. Can you wonder at this? Any severe commotion in the air can upset them.

Air-spirits help man to receive inspiration. Man imagines that all ideas and inventions, all his inspiration in the realms of art, originate with himself; he thinks of himself as the sole agent. He does not know, nor will he readily accept the idea that air-spirits can assist him in any creative art if he is ready to be helped. But when we explain that the sylphs are of the air-ether, and that the air-ether is related to man's mind; and that his mental body is influenced and affected by the air-ether, you will readily understand why air-spirits are drawn to those who use their minds, particularly in the creative arts.

Another range of little people are called 'salamanders,' and are concerned with the fire-element. They are usually small (about twelve inches high) but again can extend their size or diminish it. They are always present in the kindling flame. A little girl we know once declared she saw a little man on the hearth and that he had helped the fire to burn. She never spoke a truer word. Wherever there is a fire there is a fire-spirit bringing the flame into being. Every time you strike a match a fire-spirit is summoned. This sounds unlikely, but is true. The little man is within or behind the spark and causes the eventual flame. Those of you not clever at lighting fires should try to think and even talk kindly to the fire-elemental, saying, 'Little brother, come and help my fire to burn.' If you are friendly, and really do this from your heart, your fire will burn merrily. As you can imagine, when a huge fire is roaring away out of control the great salamanders are having a famous time.

Sometimes of course the salamanders may prove mischievous, especially if there happens to be an inharmonious condition in someone's home or in a building which houses something of a disagreeable nature. A fierce temper may very well upset the salamanders and cause them to make trouble. Any difficulties of a psychic nature in a house or building are always dangerous because they can stimulate the salamanders to activity. Salamanders can be troublesome; like children, they do not realise what they are doing. Indeed, nature-spirits are responsible for many of the phenomena thought to be produced by human spirits, and it is as well to reckon with these fun-loving little beings. If you love and accept them, and are true in yourself, they will feel a sense of responsibility, and like an animal will follow and serve you. But upset them—and be prepared for some of their jokes! Not every kind of psychic phenomenon is produced by nature-spirits, but you must remember that nature as well as human spirits dwell on the astral plane and that the former love to have fun playing with and using psychic forces.

We would stress this fact however, that all elementals, whether of earth, air, fire or water, or the astral elementals created by the evil thoughts of men, can be controlled by the one great Master, Christ. No man or woman need be troubled or hurt in any degree by an elemental entity, so long as he or she lives in the supreme light of the Christ love. There is no need to fear hauntings or unpleasant manifestations, because *you* hold the key; that key is your purity of motive, purity of life, and love for all creation.

Let us not confuse the nature-spirits and the actual fairies with some of the tiny elemental forms busily at work with the plants. These comprise a vast company not as yet on the line of evolution, and are as we have already said, the product of the creative-thought-power of some higher beings—shall we say they are created by the *minds* of the angels at the head of their particular group-soul. These angelic minds animate these elementals and direct their work, which is to assist in the growth of plants. When they have finished, they dissolve, they lose their form, fade away into the ether.

But there are true fairies, animated and directed by a group-soul, who go forward step by step towards higher forms of life. Such nature-spirits abound everywhere, except in large towns, where they dislike the harsh vibrations created by the emotions of humanity.

Nature-spirits do not suffer from sickness as humans do, but they react to violence, and they can be hurt and run away. They absorb their vital force (or nourishment, nutriment) from the emanations of the flowers—from their scent, their perfume, their colour and beauty; such is food to fairy creatures. They delight to absorb the perfume, colour and beauty of the flowers; flower spirits move gracefully, and are sometimes seen on the flowers, with gossamer clothing and wings. Yes, indeed, fairy tales are true! These beautiful creatures enjoy themselves most in a country garden, where they become attached to humans who also love flowers. Fairies work closely with such a human soul, loving its emanations.

When we say fairies dislike big cities we speak generally. You certainly won't find them hurrying along London streets, where there is nothing for them to find or serve; but they can become attached to trees in town, and can even be found in quiet town gardens. On the whole, however, to see fairies, you must go into the country, seek out the moors and hills of your beautiful Britain, for here fairy spirits abound in countless numbers. When you walk alone across the hills, or in a country lane, this is where you will become conscious of the presence of the fairies and little people, but they are very shy and timid and often if they see a human poking about they will disappear. Fairy tales describing a tiny door in the trunk of a tree into which the gnome or brownie disappears, are not without foundation, for this can happen when they want to feel safe from prying eyes.

In certain places they congregate in very large numbers. In the Pentland hills in Scotland for instance, and the moors and the hills of Devon and Cornwall. The land of the Red Indians abounds in nature-spirits, for in their long past the Indians had learnt the secret of commanding the help of the nature-spirits in growing their crops. The American Indians not only believed in but worked in harmony with the nature-spirits. We were always cognisant of the presence of our little friends and had very much to thank them for, for they can be most kind and helpful to humans; and the ideal state of the future will be when earthly man has his eyes opened to this vast unseen universe and is able to work in harmony with its inhabitants. We impress upon all the value of your individual life in the grand brotherhood of life, and how important it is for you to work in harmony, to co-operate with the angelic stream of life.

Once we said to a group in the White Eagle Lodge that we believed in everything. That may seem a sweeping statement; but what we meant—what we still mean—is that we keep an open mind upon all subjects and never say nay to anything. We are interested in and we believe in the strangest things, because there is so much in heaven and earth which is undreamed of in the philosophy of man.

VII

FAIRY TALES

The elementals and fairy creatures which abound in the life of nature are all intimately concerned with man's spiritual evolution, with his joys and his appreciation of nature's beauty. It is therefore necessary for the soul advancing on the spiritual path to become aware of these invisible helpers at some stage of his journey. Many concentrate their whole attention on human survival, while their consciousness of the little people, the nature-spirits, is quite closed. They are totally unaware of these little brothers, and their knowledge of the world of spirit is thus limited. At a certain point on the path of unfoldment man's vision clears and he becomes conscious of his little brethren all around him.

We have already spoken about the four elements, and have explained that interpenetrating the four physical elements is a finer ether not perceptible by physical sense but which can be registered by that sixth sense of man, the intuition, or the 'psychic' sense. It is from the substance of this finer ether within the four elements that fairy people are created, and thus these etheric creatures can be registered by the *etheric* vision of man. For instance, this finer ether, which is interpenetrating the earth and the earth-ether, is the substance from which the little people called gnomes, the spirits of the earth, are created.

There is a water-ether, a substance behind and within physical water substance, and from that water-ether are created those spirits called undines or water-spirits. So also with the fire and the air; from the element of fire, the fire-ether, are created the salamanders whose work is to bring live fire into manifestation. Within the ether of each element, and created from it, dwell the creatures associated with that element.

The air is full of the creatures associated with the air-element and created of the air-ether, some quite small, some larger than men. Especially are they to be found among mountains. If you go into the high and solitary places far from human contacts, there you will become aware of the presence of the mountain-spirits, sylphs or the air-spirits. They are powerful and mysterious, and do not always welcome the intrusion of man. As an instance we would cite the mysterious difficulties sometimes experienced by mountaineers. The spirits of the air do not suffer man's physical intrusion beyond a certain point.

Wonderful spirit-beings such as these inhabit the finer ethers. In your meditations you can, if you work hard, penetrate these heights or these inner worlds. That is what you are endeavouring to do; not in your physical but in your astral body you can visit the settlements of the fairy people; you can see their fairy palaces *within* the earth, *inside* the mountains.

All these finer states of life interpenetrate your physical life. You see matter as a solid mass and find it difficult to believe there can be another life within this apparent solidity. You forget that matter is really only loosely knit and can be interpenetrated by other forms of matter, vibrating at different rates. This is why we can take you to fairy settlements within the substance of the earth, fairy palaces built from beautiful material similar in appearance to alabaster. We can take you into fairy gardens existing within your own physical gardens. In your meditations you can go into the depths of the ocean bed and find *within* the water settlements of the spirits of the water, the undines.

You can go to the seashore, to all places where there is an abundance of water and vegetation growing in water and there in the etheric counterpart of the water you will find your little nature-spirits or undines.

Now we would like you to think of the four elements and realise that each of these elements exists also within your own being; therefore you can draw the little people of all the elements to yourself, especially at times when you are undergoing the initiations which we have described on other occasions.

You who are students of occultism will perhaps be familiar with some of the initiations through which the candidates in the Egyptian, the Greek and other ancient mystery schools were taken. These initiations were indicative of the tests that come to man to try the qualities of his soul related to every one of the four elements. The beings native to each element are concerned with these initiations on the inner or soul plane.

For instance, when man is undergoing experiences which test his emotions, the spirits of the water, the undines will be involved; in the initiations of the air, when the mental bodies are being strengthened, you will find the sylphs will be your servants. In the initiation of earth when the soul is learning to free itself from the bondage of matter, surrendering self-will and the lower nature, the elementals of the earth are concerned. The fire-spirits or spirits of the sun are concerned with your soul when it is learning the lesson of love.

Another aspect of this subject which we will touch on is the part which fairies play in your folklore and fairy stories. For remember, many of these stories handed down to you from ages past, are stories about man's soul experiences. We come also into the realms of magic, for all magic is largely dependent on the nature-spirits. We are thinking now of stories which tell of certain articles having attached to them a fairy or elemental being who, when commanded, obeys the owner of that article: the story of the slave of the lamp, for instance, or the slave of the ring. These stories have truth in them. Amulets or tokens which the ancients used would often have an elemental attached, for these creatures of the nature kingdom can be commanded and enslaved by occultists, priests or magicians, who understand the laws of the etheric world.

We would point out however that those who have the power to command the help of nature-spirits must also possess a measure of true spiritual development, otherwise a penalty will be exacted. An adept, for instance, lives in harmony with natural law, and the nature-spirits therefore work with him. You will remember how readily the Master Jesus controlled the nature-spirits of the water and the air during a storm at sea. They had no choice but to obey him because he was an adept, a master. But an occultist with a certain knowledge but lacking this true power of command will perhaps bargain with an elemental, saying, 'I will serve you, if you will first serve me.' As in the story of Faust, he will sell his very soul in order that these nature-spirits will obey him. But afterwards the reckoning must come, and he in turn must serve the nature-spirits.

The little people attached to jewels or other articles will serve the wearer who loves and treats them kindly. We would impress on you that the fundamental law of life is love, and the gnomes look up to mankind and expect goodness and love from them. They like to emulate humans, and will clothe themselves in the same way as those around them, creating not only a dress but a personality. For instance in China the elementals will apparently be Chinese. They will dress in Chinese clothes and their customs will be similar to those of the land in which they live. The little people who served the Indians were not English! They looked and dressed like the Indians. It is the same with all countries. The human family has a responsibility towards the elementals, and human love is important to them—love and goodness and purity of life.

What do we find when human nature becomes depraved? We find it results in the creation of etheric creatures quite different from and lower than the elementals of the four ethers. The emanations from a man who indulges in cruelty or who gives free rein to the gross appetites of the body, create elementals which can readily be seen. We will give an illustration: those poor people who become saturated by alcohol fall into a state of delirium, and in that delirium they see very unpleasant creatures—these are not hallucinations, but are elemental forms created from the emanations of the alcoholic.

Those people who give way to violent passion create creatures of a different nature again, for their passion creates quite an army of what you would call little 'devils.' They are creatures of about twelve to eighteen inches high, sometimes black, sometimes fiery red, with horns and tail, which can be seen, heard and felt by the sensitive. A common saying refers to 'so-and-so' having a 'devil.' Many a true word is spoken in jest! Depression also will create elementals which will cling to the one who creates them; indeed, any violent emotions create elementals out of the lower ethers comprising your own being. Similarly, harmonious and aspiring thoughts create delicate, charming and happy little people who will work for you, and for those around you.

When people begin to understand what they are creating by their thoughts and their actions and their emotions, they will perhaps understand the great need for discipline in their life.

You are all aware that there are two aspects of human nature. There is that part of man which clings to the earth, the nature desirous of satisfying physical appetites. If this nature, this physical appetite, is allowed to take precedence over the part of the nature which is spiritual, the individual is said to be in the grip of the enemy of man's spirit. When, however, the spirit, the higher self, is able to rise supreme over the lower desires, then the soul is winning through and passing its tests.

Most fairy stories are concerned with these two parts of man's nature, the material and the spiritual. In more advanced stories you will discern the transmuting of the lower nature by the light, or the solar or creative force. Such myths and fairy stories are designed to teach the uninitiated how this solar force can be stimulated and directed outwards in the form of light and spiritual power to help others.

In these stories the king is often a central character. Very often they begin, 'Once upon a time a king had a beautiful daughter . . .' Various princes or noblemen journeyed from far lands to win the hand of this princess. The king would say to these princes, 'My daughter shall be given to him who will bring me the golden apple'—or some other coveted prize. This wonderful thing of rare beauty was always hidden at the end of a long journey across mountains, through dark woods, across broad rivers. If the prince wanted to claim the princess as his bride he had to be tested for certain qualities of character. Every one of these tests which the princes were required to undergo indicates an initiation. For instance, the dark wood in which all kinds of creatures lurked indicates the world of the lower or astral desires which could ensnare them. To overcome this temptation they needed to have great courage and to keep their vision on their goal. They had neither to be led astray, nor to be overcome by fear.

Some of you, either in meditation, or in dreams may find yourselves in such a wood, confronted by fierce animals. When you can overcome your fear of them they cannot hurt you. These experiences are tests of the soul, tests for courage on the astral plane. Fear is one of the greatest enemies of men, so the soul has to learn to discard all fear. If you will think for a moment you will know that fear in some form or another is the greatest enemy in life. People live dominated by fear—fear of the future, fear of ill health, of death, of losing their property, of starvation, of loss. Countless fears beset mankind. Thus the great test which the initiate had to overcome was that of fear in many subtle forms.

The princes seeking the hand of the princess might have to face some fiery dragon. The fiery dragon indicates the lower nature. In other words, the solar fire, the creative fires which dwell in man can appear in frightening forms and threaten to overwhelm the life. When the fiery nature is not controlled, it causes men and women sometimes to do terrible things. Once it is controlled, it is raised into the heart as love and into the head as divine intelligence. When complete control is lacking it comes out in bad temper. But once this light, this life force rises into the heart, it manifests as great warmth of love, sweetness and sympathy. When raised to the head centre, having been transmuted from the lower nature, it is symbolised by the halo to be seen about the heads of saints or by the golden crown. Gold in mythology always represents this love, this divine solar force. Silver, on the other hand, is symbolic of the intellect. We do not decry development of the intellect which can, and indeed must become a channel for the divine intelligence; but we would explain that the intellect must be used in the right way and must not dominate the wisdom of the heart. The wisdom of the heart is gold; the brilliance of the intellect is silver. When the two are perfectly balanced, then comes divine intelligence and spiritual completion—if there is such a thing— and control and triumph over the lower nature.

The prince in our story might have to cross a roaring river or meet a storm at sea. You who have listened so often to these talks will know that here we have the emotional nature depicted, for the prince also has to triumph over his unruly emotions. You will find that all these fairy stories are concerned with four elements, earth, air, fire and water, which, as we have said, also symbolise the four great initiations. The prince meets tests in all these elements. The earth stands as the last initiation because it symbolises complete triumph over the earth man, the birth of the Christ man. When our prince has gone through all these four tests he is ready for his marriage to the princess.

So many of the old fairy stories run in this way and really recount the story of the spiritual evolution and development of the soul. At the end of each comes the mystical marriage, the marriage between the soul and the spirit. The soul having battled with its foes, overcome the lower nature and become purified, is at last ready for complete union with the higher self.

There is another story we would like to speak of. Have you not a story of a little princess, the great joy of her royal parents, at whose christening fairies gave the gifts of beauty and riches and all the good things which any little girl would like to have? After the good fairies had gone, a bad fairy arrived on the scene. The parents were told at a certain time in the life of the child there was likely to be a catastrophe. The frightened parents did everything they could to protect the child from this happening, but without avail.

A great lesson lies here. You see, the whole point is that the soul is destined to go through certain experiences for its spiritual progress.

So the princess had the injury and fell asleep. We suggest that the material side of life claimed and enchained that soul. You are all like that princess. If you could see your real selves, you would be amazed, because your real self is as beautiful as we are told the princess was. Above you, away from the earth, the princess, your higher self, dwells. In most people that beautiful princess, the higher self, has been injured by worldliness, many incarnations back, and has fallen into an enchanted sleep. Sometimes it takes a long time for that self to be awakened, and the one thing which has the power to awaken the princess, or the higher self, is love.

Thus the higher self sleeps until the time is ready. Sometimes the princess lies sleeping in a castle overgrown with poisonous weeds. Is that not like conditions here in the world? The material world seems to fasten itself around the soul as it slumbers. Often you see only a rough exterior to a man or woman, but if only you could cut away the rough exterior you would find a very sweet and beautiful nature lying sleeping beneath. That, beloved children, is

89

your work, our work, to seek always for the
princess hidden behind all that prickly growth.
It is no easy task! All have the light within; all
have that higher princess self. It is our work in
the world to deal with each other lovingly,
always seeing the best, seeking to uncover that
beauty, encouraging it in every possible way.

You will notice, if you have contacted your
Master in meditation, that he will always be
patient and kind, never harsh, never sitting in
judgment on you, never forcing you, always
trying to draw out from you your true nature.
By this test you can know your teacher and
guide, because teachers from the spirit will be
loving and always see the best. Don't make any
mistake, guides and teachers do not flatter.
But they see the best in you, they draw out your
higher nature. As the soul evolves it is able to
discern the beauty both in its teacher and in the
spiritual vista which lies before it.

Is there not another story of a little girl who
was a victim of a witch and ran away and
became lost in the wood? The princess had fled
from her castle because an evil stepmother had
tried to poison her (which illustrates how the
evil aspect tries to poison the good).

This story really concerns man's higher self
when it becomes separated from the lower by

the shadow of what is called evil. The child of light goes forth into the wilderness or wood to learn, to gain experience. She goes in search of truth. We might liken this wood to the wilderness in which the frightened soul wanders on the earth. The soul, or the child, the little girl, is met by gnomes who befriend her. These dwarfs are the qualities of the soul represented by the signs of the Zodiac. She lives for a long time happily with the dwarfs in the wood, and then come the dark forces, the evil forces trying to destroy, trying to poison mind and body. It is interesting that the same symbolism is employed as is found in Genesis. The little princess is tempted to eat an apple and it is her undoing; she falls into a deep sleep or death. Is this not continually happening to you all? The evil of the world would extinguish your true self, but does not quite succeed. Evil cannot wholly kill the soul. The soul remains in a state of imprisonment which looks like death, until the time is right for the prince to come. This does not take place over the span of a few months or even a few years, but can extend through many lives. The soul sleeps, waiting. Then at the right moment the prince comes to awaken the sleeping princess. Here is symbolised the mystical marriage of soul and spirit.

Beloved brethren, we have spoken to you very simply, as children, but profound truths are so simple that often man in his arrogance, overlooks the truth. His brain and intellect is so powerful, he is unaware of the one simple thing which could solve the whole problem of his life on earth . . . the kiss of the Son, the awakening of love, the Christ spirit in his heart.

Now be happy, be filled with joy and look forward into the light. Go straight to the golden heart of love, and know that all is well. Live and move in that golden eternal light, and then nothing can hurt you. The only reality is the light, is God, is love.

VIII

IN HARMONY WITH LIFE

Certain people, it is said, possess the 'green finger.' Their vibration harmoniously attracts innumerable nature-spirits; they can win the co-operation and interest of their little nature brethren. Others have not developed this aspect of their being. They may say they love flowers and they may do so, up to a point; but remember that love means unwavering service, and really to love growing things means to put oneself in harmony with their very lifestream. Some may not be able to do all this because they are developing other aspects of their sevenfold God-nature at the present time; but perfected man will have the gift of controlling the nature world, and of calling the nature-spirits to action and service.

Love your flowers, my brethren; talk to them, and talk to your brother trees. The Red Indian used to talk to the spirit of the trees, and the flowers, to the running water; he talked to the Great Spirit in the mountains—all life manifested the Great White Spirit to him. Be friendly with your little field daisies, with the flowers of the hedgerows, even with the very blades of grass. Try to feel the brotherhood you share with every living creature. Even the minerals are alive with the light of God. Each wayside stone is vibrating with a light and life it shares with every plant that grows. If you had clear vision, you would see that all the flowers and trees in your garden are pulsating, vibrating with colour and life.

The earth is imbued with the divine fire of life. This divine fire, which is also called love, is the life in everything. If your vision were clear, you would see the divine fire even within inanimate things; metal, stones, wood, are all pulsating with tiny sparks of light, of fire. All nature is pulsating with this divine life.

The colours in the flowers are brought to them by the fairies, the nature-spirits, who are working through the central stems of the plants, pouring in their own essence according to the need of the flowers. In other words, the flower is taking upon itself the colour of the fairy creature working with it; the essence, the quality of the consciousness of the fairy, is being expressed through the particular flower.

If you could look at a tree with your spiritual eyes open you would see more than its trunk, limbs and foliage. You would see the fire within the earth and in the roots of the tree; you would see the fire rising up through the trunk of the tree to radiate light through all its branches and leaves, particularly in the spring of the year. The divine fire is shining not only in the sky, in the rays of the sun, but in the earth itself and in all nature.

Not only is this inner or etheric world vibrating with colour, sound and perfume, but interpenetrating all are the rays of the planets. Certain parts of your body vibrate in harmony with certain planets, for every planet has its correspondence in the being of man. Try to understand and receive these vibrations more fully into your being. When you have learnt to vibrate in tune with all life, you will have attained mastership.

We would raise you out of the personal, beyond the limitations of the present earth consciousness into the eternal life.

Use your heavenly imagination and come with us in spirit to a temple where we all kneel about the altar. The arch of the temple receives the golden stream from the sun. Do

you see that the golden life-stream is more than
sunlight? Look—it is life itself, it is charged
with life-essence, with tiny specks of life whirl-
ing in space. Now we see these tiny specks
manifesting in some lower form of life on earth,
we realise we are all linked to these tiny specks
of life, our younger brethren of the mineral,
vegetable and animal kingdoms. . . .

As you gaze upon and find yourself caught
up in this golden life-stream, attune yourself to
the music of the spheres of spiritual life, and as
you listen, you will hear their harmonies
sounding in your heart.

Listen . . . listen deeply. . . .

You are now bathed in colour of the most
exquisitely delicate shades. You are in the
spirit world, and countless beings move about
you in the radiance of the spiritual sunlight.

By their particular colour and note of harmony we recognise the planetary angels who
are at work upon and within our own being.
Each must learn to recognise the influence of
the planetary angel most closely associated with
him in his present life. When we have learnt
this, we shall be better channels for service to
our younger brethren. On the higher plane each
attracts the planetary angels whose particular
help our soul needs in any one incarnation.

As the psychic centres of man's being are vivified, so humanity will begin to respond consciously, with understanding and intelligence, to these planetary angels, and when this becomes a general practice, another golden age will dawn.

According to your birth into matter in this incarnation, you, the ego, have been linked to particular planets, and teachers from these planets are in contact with your higher self. This was all arranged long before physical conception took place. Before a child is born certain magnetic and spiritual currents are directed to the chosen parents, which are linked with the planetary forces brought to play upon the soul. The links which bring parent and child together were forged in the previous incarnation, for the soul is sent from the centre of life under the direction of the Lords of Karma.

The 'seven angels round the throne' spoken of by John in his Revelation, concern this very truth, for the 'seven angels round the throne' are the planetary beings, great Lords of the Flame who hold all incarnating souls within their vision; each soul returns to earth with the planetary forces already concentrated upon it.

Certain influences are bound to affect the

life and mould its conditions and circumstances; but as well as these planetary forces there is also the higher power, that sacred flame which burns brighter than any planetary light which strikes the ego. This central light is the sun of man's being and it is centred in the heart. As the heart-centre develops during the course of evolution, angels from each planet will attend the candidate to help him on his soul path.

You have little idea yet of the stupendous organisation of the spiritual life, and when the great Teacher said, 'Are not five sparrows sold for two farthings? and not one of them is forgotten before God. But even the very hairs of your head are all numbered,' this was no exaggerated statement. Life is so perfectly organised and planned, that every step is noted and recorded. Not only actions but also aspirations and thoughts are recorded, as well as the effect of thoughts and actions upon those who cross and re-cross your path of life.

The physical body is constructed under the direction of planetary angels and moulded by the planetary influences brought to bear upon it. Every disease of the body is traceable to planetary—which is, in effect, karmic—matter. Every sign of the Zodiac is related to a particular part of the physical body, and every planet is related to one or other of the higher vehicles or spiritual bodies of man. Each spiritual or finer body is related, connected or attached to one or other of the seven psychic or sacred centres of the body.

These inner truths of the planetary angels and the forces at play upon the soul were well known to the ancients, for in the beginning of life on this earthplane, these planetary beings were visible to the humans and they were regarded as God-men, beings sent from God. As man withdrew into the extreme darkness of physical matter, he lost sight of these angelic hierarchies. But as he returns on the upward arc of evolution, and as the seven lights in his body radiate to show him where he is in the great scheme of life, then he will see with full recognition these planetary angels who are concerned with his evolution and his return in full consciousness to God his Father-Mother.

In the beginning was the Word; it was the vibration which caused the Light. The Light was the Son, the first-born of the Father. Within the Light is all-life; and the Light is divided into seven rays; on the seven rays of colour within the Light come the planetary angelic messengers to serve the human race. And when you direct or concentrate certain colours for the healing of your brethren you will, if you are working correctly, link up with the angels of that ray.

The angels work from certain planes or spheres in the world of spirit directing their love upon the earth plane. They work through groups, even to the tiny forms of life on the earth. We mean by this that the *instinctive* mind of the lower forms of life works under the control and direction of one of these great angels. Thus an animal will respond instinctively to the controlling influence of the mind of the group; and the mind of the group of the animal is under the love and wisdom of an angel. So also with primitive humanity. It is only when we come to the more highly evolved of the human family that we discern freewill to any degree. The angels who direct the group-mind serve under the direction of one of the seven great ones round the throne, round the central light, the First Great Cause . . . God.

From the one central point, the First Great Cause, are sent forth countless millions of life lines, like little fine capillaries; perhaps we could almost liken the great cosmic scheme of life to the human circulation, in a certain way.

Every ray of life is in perfect association, is perfectly linked with the central Cause. There is nothing haphazard in creation, all is perfection —perfect rhythm, perfect form, exactness in every detail. Think for a moment of the beauty of the colour and texture of the butterfly's wings, and reflect that in order to see its full beauty you need to look through a microscope, and to focus a clearer, more powerful light upon it. Likewise with the tiniest wild flower that grows. Take a tiny starlike flower, and place it under a microscope, and you will see it as a jewel, you will see all the colours of the rainbow reflected in its petals, and if you are attuned to the harmonies of the spheres of light, you will hear them sounding from the beauty of that little flower.

Look for beauty in your everyday life. Do not take things for granted. Look for the exquisite beauty in flowers, in the sunlight, in the dewdrop. If you can, go out in the early morning when the dew is still wet upon the grass and bejewelling the gossamer cobwebs. Gaze upon the beauty and the intricacy of the construction of the little webs—and then feel, stirring within you, a sense of brotherhood, of kinship with that beautiful thing.

A brother of the Great White Lodge is

aware of his relationship to all forms of life. He can identify himself with the tiniest insect, with the flowers, sunlight and the gentle rains. This is the way, my brethren. This is the way all must pass into the Temple. 'Flower in the crannied wall,' says your poet, 'If I could understand thy life, I should understand God and the universe.' And you *can* understand: not with your mind alone, but through identifying yourself with the light and with the life-streams, and becoming at one with the vibration of the Sun or of God.

Endeavour as you look on any physical form to look *into* that form and to the spirit. See it in the very roots of the trees, in the trunk, branches and the leaves. See the white light rising as the sap rises. See this phenomenon taking place in the flowers and bushes and trees and all nature. Look always for the spirit behind or within all form. Become *en rapport* with this God-life in everything. Realise it in the air you breathe, in the water you drink and bathe in; see it in the sky, in the winds, in the air; see it in the fire. Cultivate this inner gift; call it, if you like, imagination, but remember that imagination is the bridge which will take man across physical matter into the etheric and indeed into the celestial world. By using this gift you can help yourselves and all mankind. It will create harmony in you and beauty in your lives, for you will have realms revealed to you, of which you know nothing at the present time.

Learn therefore to step outside your personality, or your self as a limiting and confining thing; get away from yourself, and the limitations of the physical brain, learn to slip away on the wings of imagery. You will find yourself free, and in this land of meditation, which is the real land of light, you will see behind the scenes of physical life, and in so doing you will learn the true meaning of brotherhood; you will learn that you cannot serve with all your heart and soul and mind without growing in Christ-likeness. You will know that you in no wise can separate yourself from the great ocean of life; you cannot harm your brother, whether of the vegetable, animal or human kingdom, without yourself being hurt.

We come back again to the simple teaching of Jesus the Son and the Light: 'Little children, love one another. . . . *Love one another.*'

Brethren, we have met together in love, and in love we shall separate, but always will the chain of love bind us heart to heart. May you love one another and all the great brotherhood of life. Be patient and tolerant with each other's human faults, and in time they will fade, and you will know each other as you are known in heaven, just, perfect and true brothers of the Light.

SUBJECT INDEX

The White Eagle Publishing Trust, which publishes and distributes the White Eagle teaching, is part of the wider work of the White Eagle Lodge, an undenominational Christian church, founded in 1936 to give practical expression to the White Eagle teaching. Here men and women may come to learn the reason for their life on earth and how to serve and live in harmony with the whole brotherhood of life, visible and invisible, in health and happiness. Readers wishing to know more of the work of the White Eagle Lodge may write to the General Secretary, White Eagle Lodge, New Lands, Liss, Hampshire, GU33 7HY; or can call at the White Eagle Lodge, 9 St Mary Abbots Place, London W8 6LS.

THE WHITE EAGLE PUBLISHING TRUST

NEW LANDS · LISS · HAMPSHIRE